10 BEST
Artistic Nude
Photo Manips
by Larry Murk

Preface

I, Larry Murk, graduated from Stanford University in 1987 with a bachelors degree in computer science. In 2000 I suffered an accident that caused a spinal cord injury leaving me a quadriplegic. Luckily I can still control my arms enough to operate a computer reasonably. I have always been interested in art and being confined to a wheelchair has led me to explore the world of digital image creation. My image editor of choice is named GIMP. GIMP is very similar to Photoshop except that it is FREE so I highly recommend everyone try it out.

Every image in this book was created by my editing a photograph. In each case I was given permission to create a video tutorial showing how I altered the photograph. Visit the ClassicsGold Youtube channel to view videos of how each painting was created. The video will supply links to the original photo, the model and the photographer (when available). The ebook version of this book has hyperlinks for easy navigation.

I hope you enjoy sharing these images as much as I enjoyed creating them.

All pictures are original works created by the author Larry Murk. These works are copyrighted and may not be redistributed or sold without the express written authorization of Larry Murk.

WARNING: This book contains images with nudity and is recommended for ADULTS.

Naked Sacrifice

Her naked body lies motionless across the blue planet as a sacrifice to the ominous heavens above.

Photographer: Huit Photography
Model: Katlyn

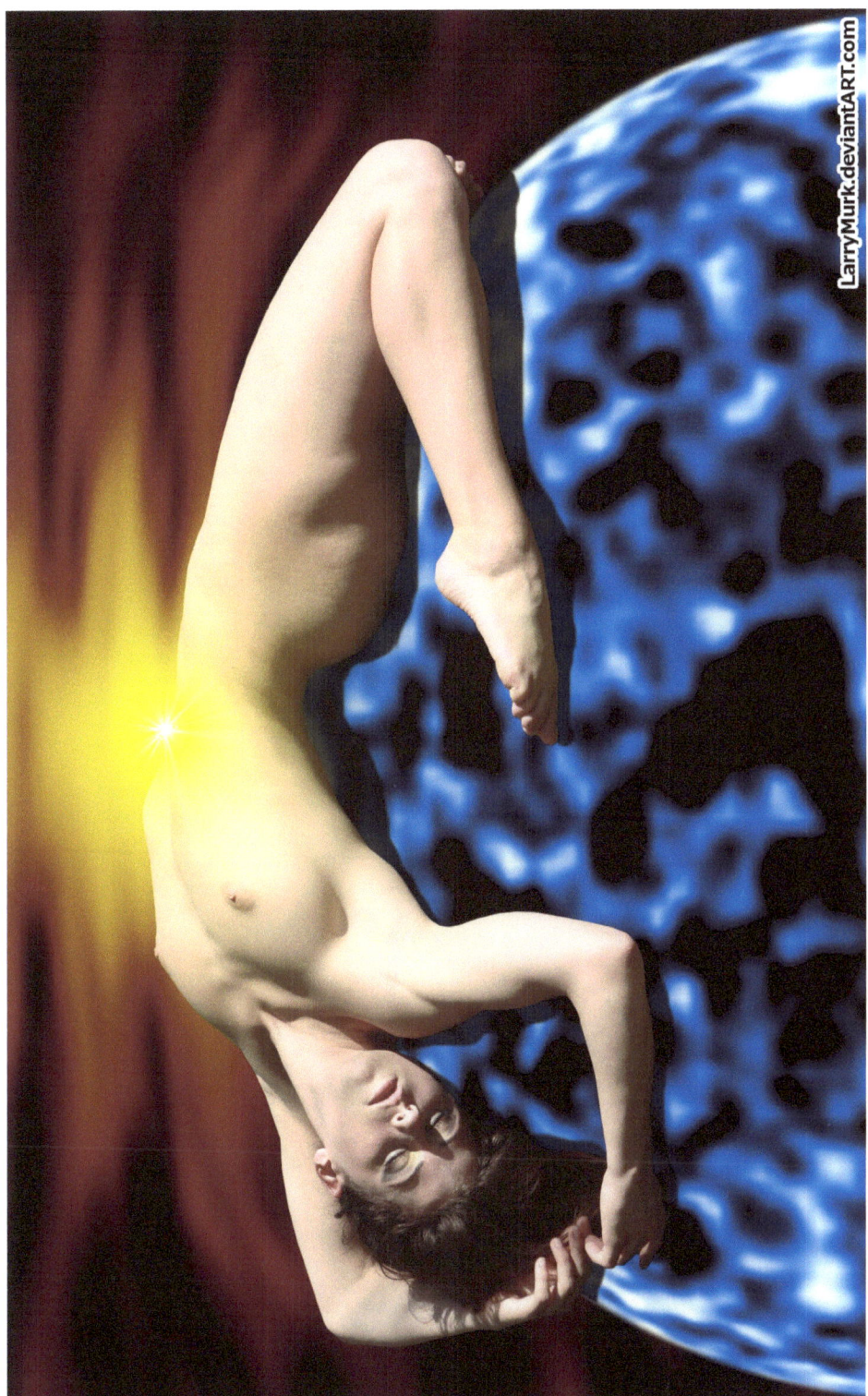

Squeaky Clean

Running one hand through her hair she dreams of her squeaky clean body showering amidst bubbling cleansing water.

Photographer: Barry of DGIConcepts
Model: Carolyn

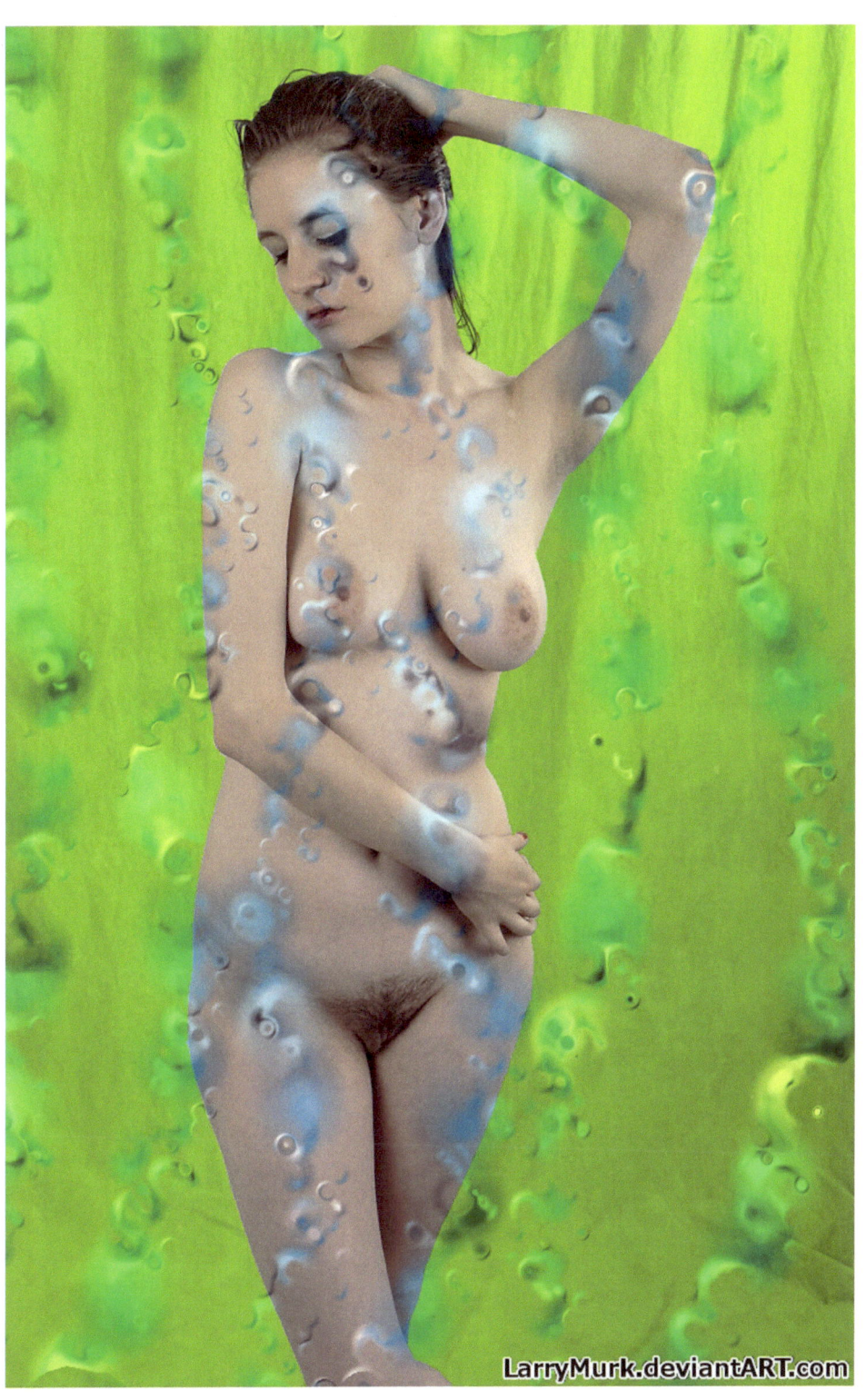

Dirty Girl

This dirty girl feels perfectly at home resting in a pool of muddy water.

Photographer: Barry of DGIConcepts
Model: Starr

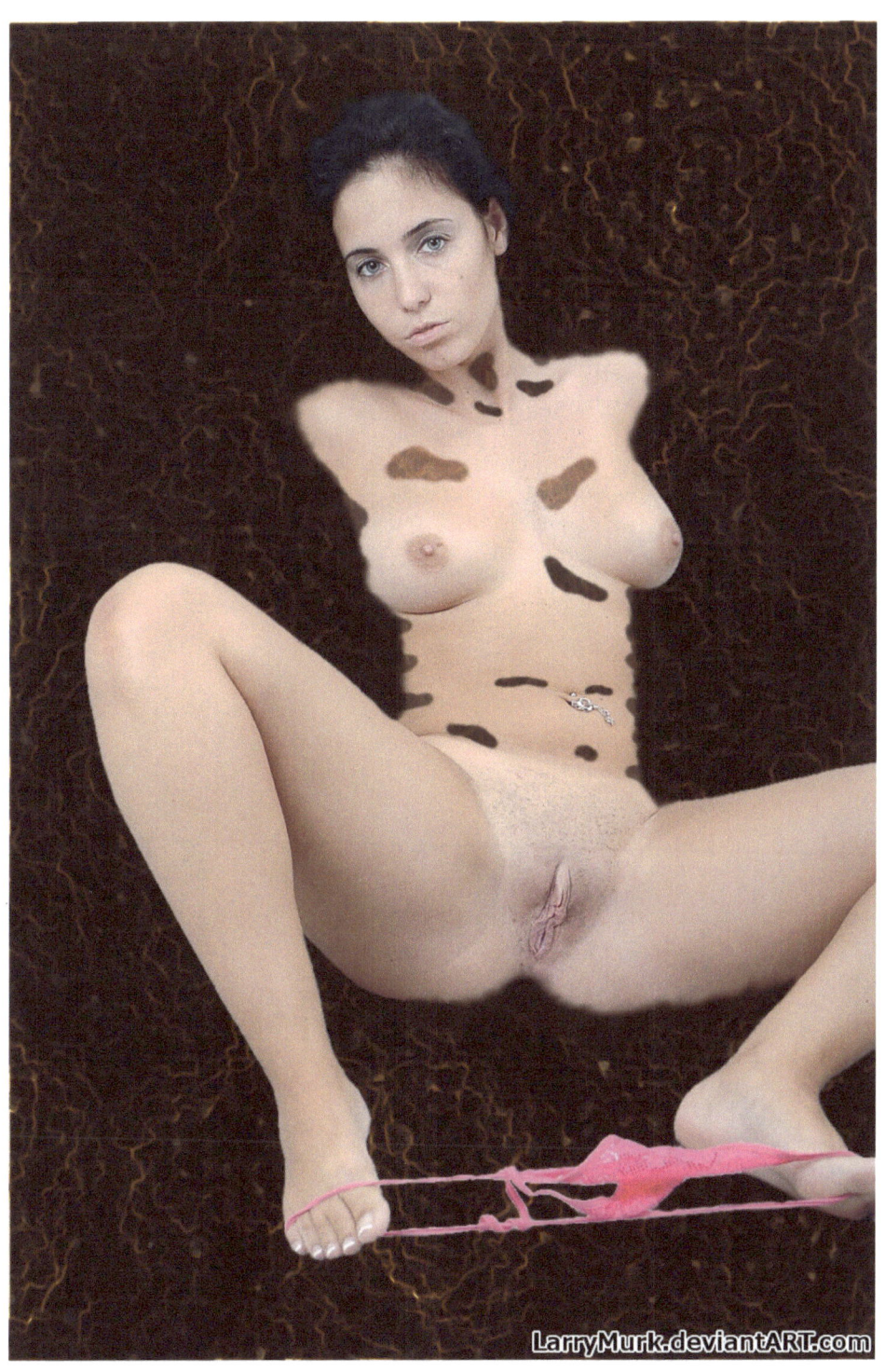

Floating in the Clouds

Clouds gently lift her painted body high into the heavens where only the angels can admire her tinted beauty.

Photographer: Rasmus
Model: Chrissi

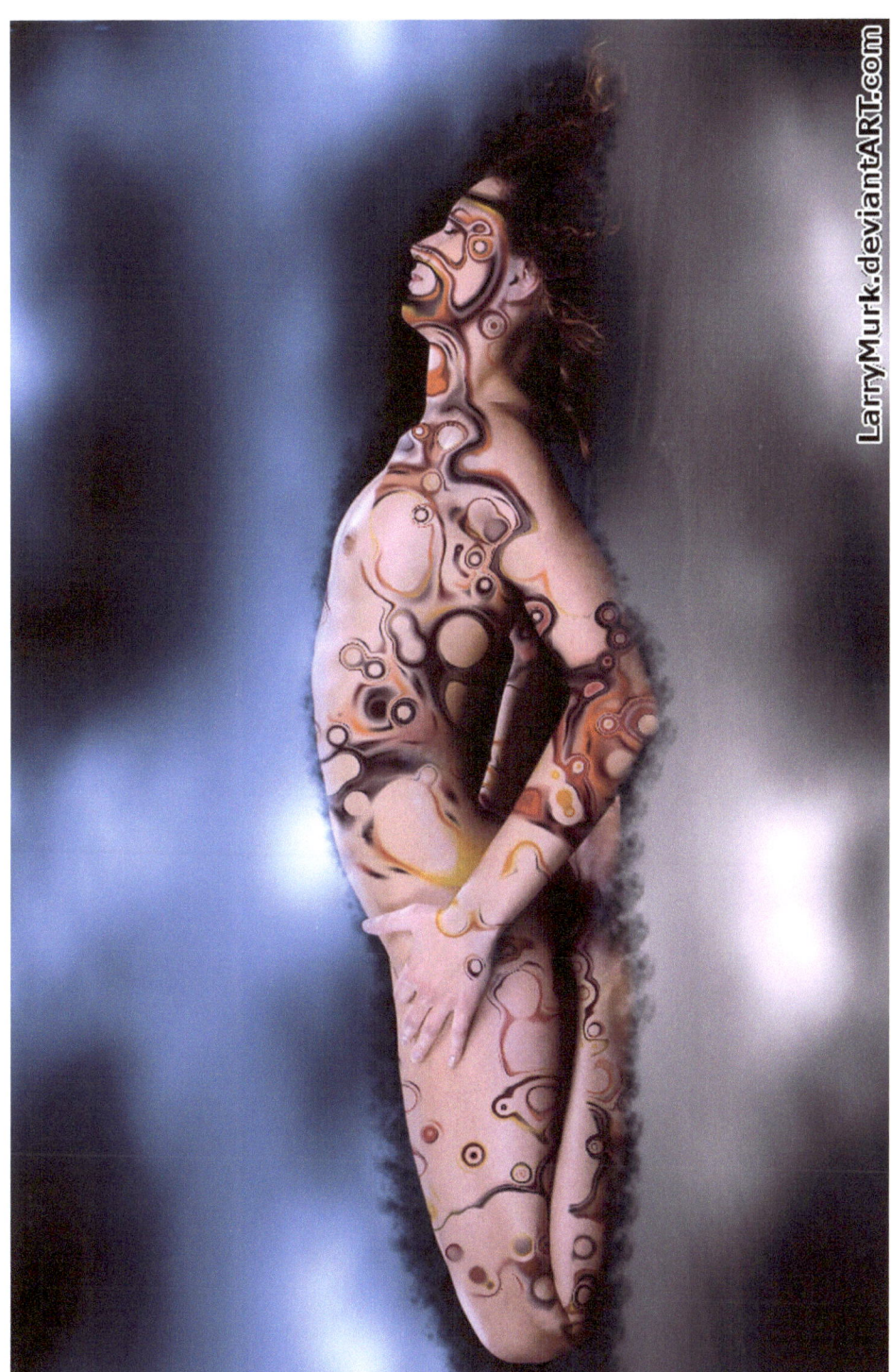

Pink Marble Statue

Frozen in time, blood and skin morphed into the timeless pink marble statue posing upon a lonely white pedestal.

Photographer: t-model
Model: Manny

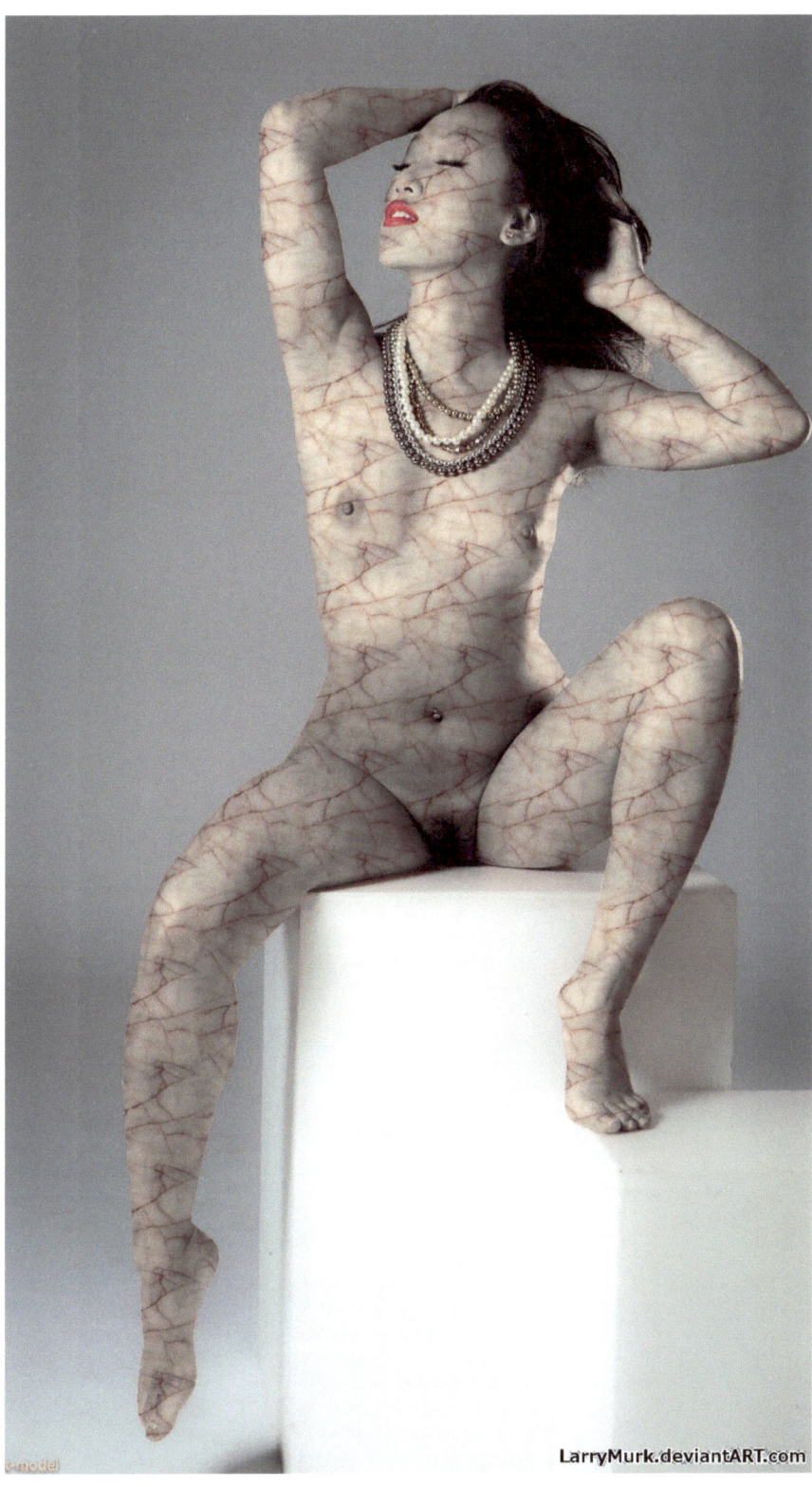

Wrapped in Red Neon Light

Body bound by a band of red neon light, there is no escaping the scorching sun rays attacking her defenseless, vulnerable skin.

Photographer: Henry Choi
Model: Jodie

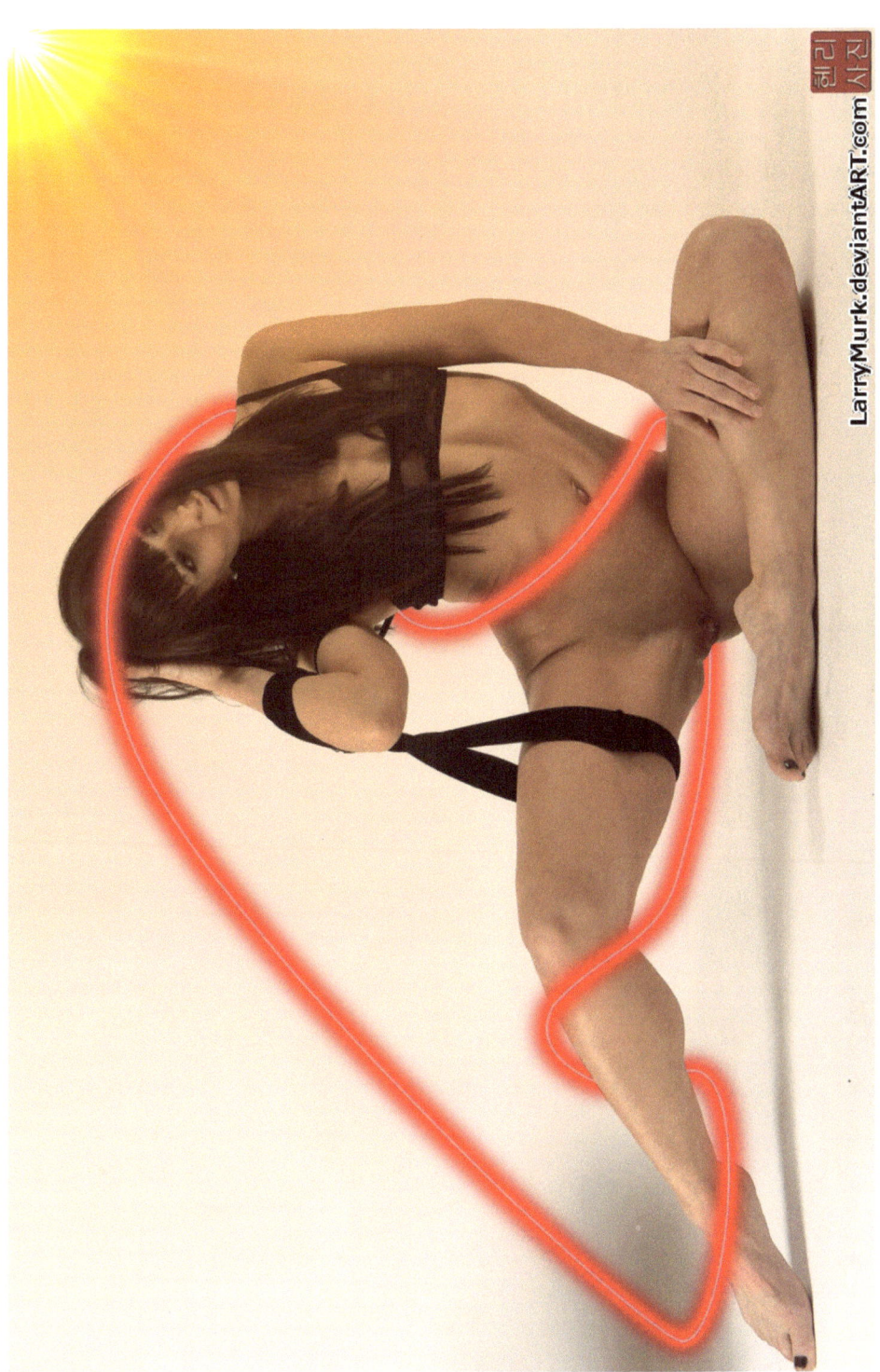

Splattered in Paint

Even the stylish black leather jacket couldn't guard her exposed flesh from speckles of red, yellow and blue paint splattered recklessly.

Photographer: Pierre of Easy-Shutter
Model: Elana

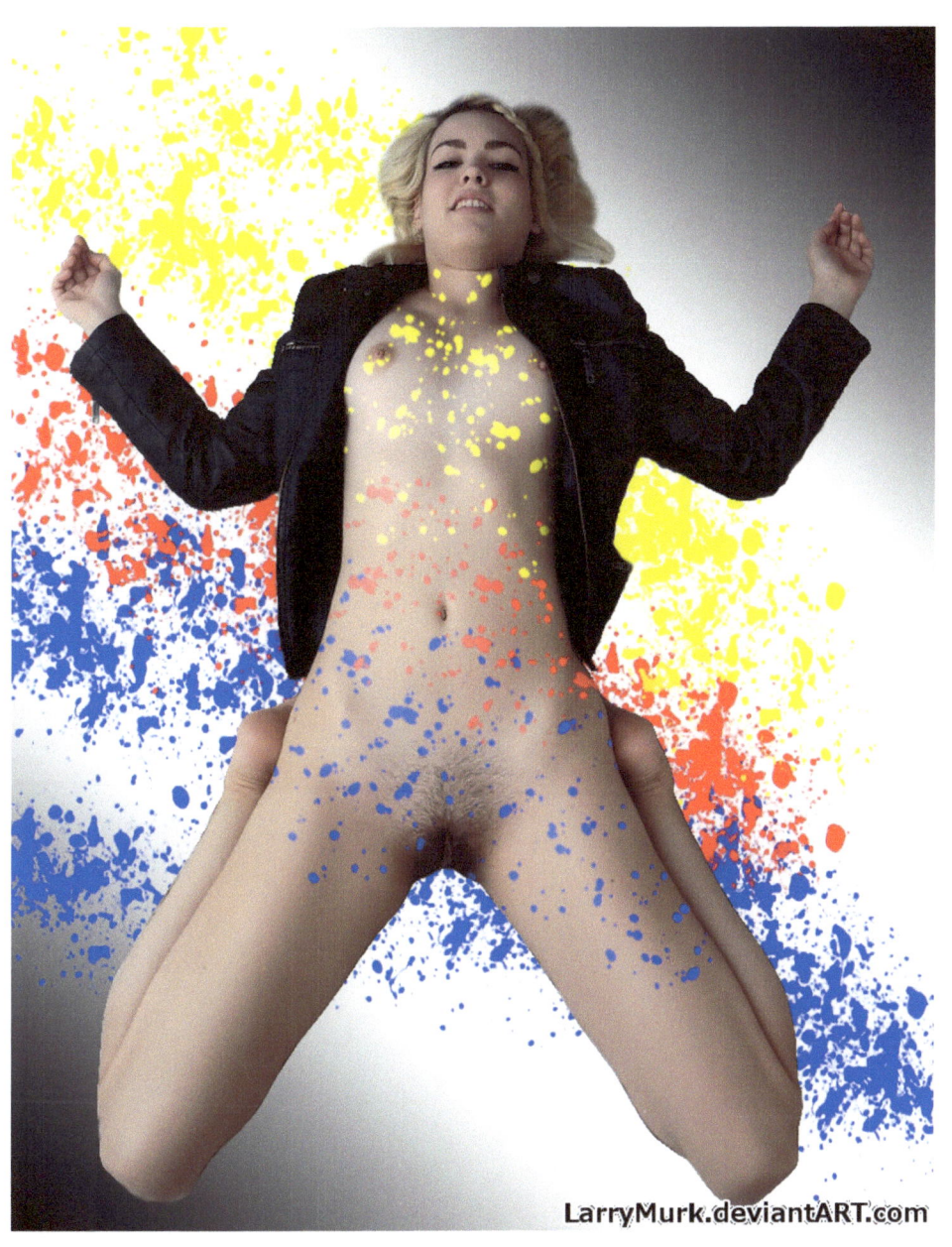

Cardboard Nude in Flower Bed

Daisies of every color populating this flower bed backdrop snicker over the irony of this curvy nude goddess printed onto flat cardboard.

Photographer: Jon Mann
Model: Danielle Trixie

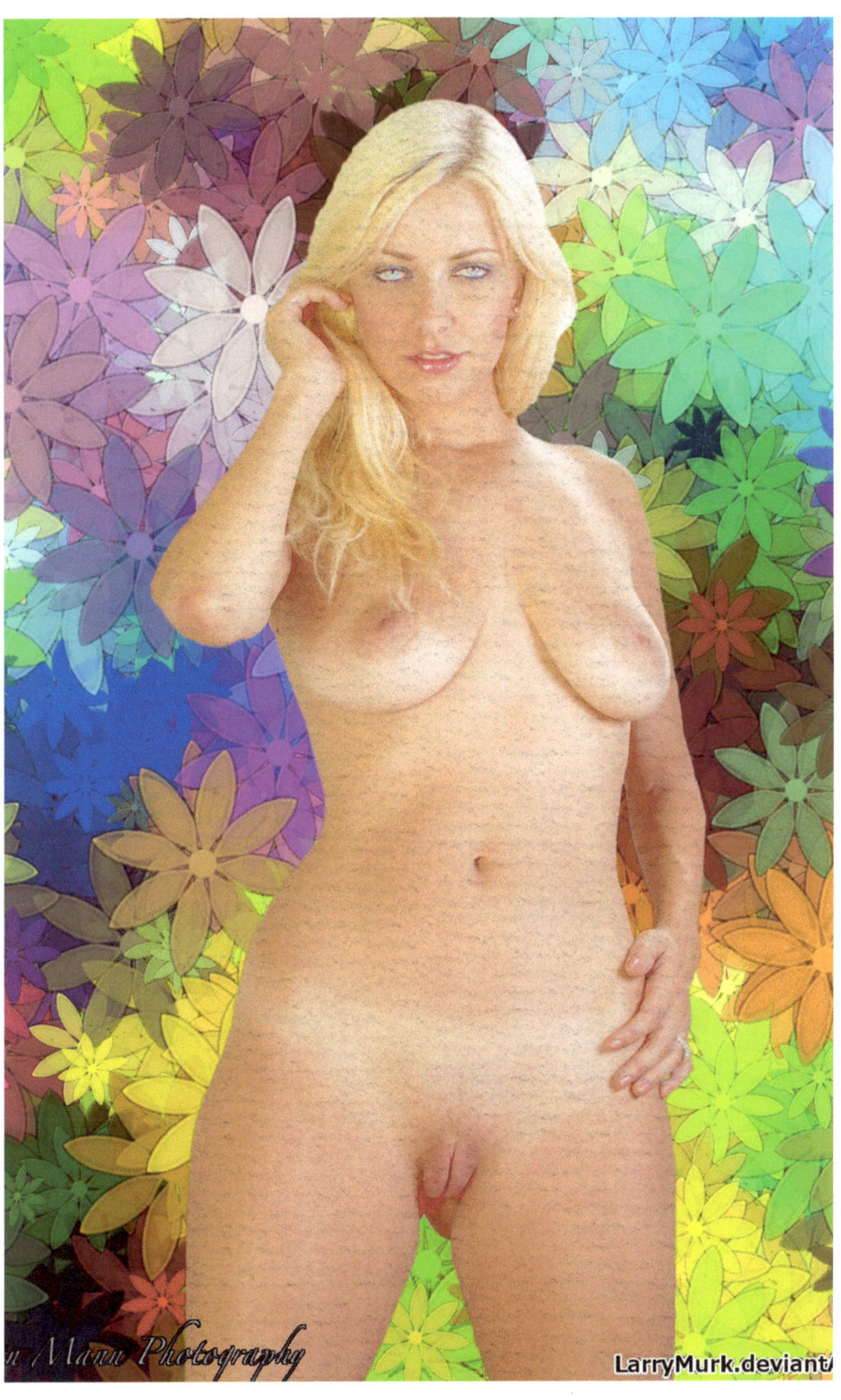

Kickin' Back on Neon Stairs

This devilish stare suggests that a leisurely afternoon kicking back on neon stairs might turn into something more.

Photographer: 3kmanos
Model: Adriana

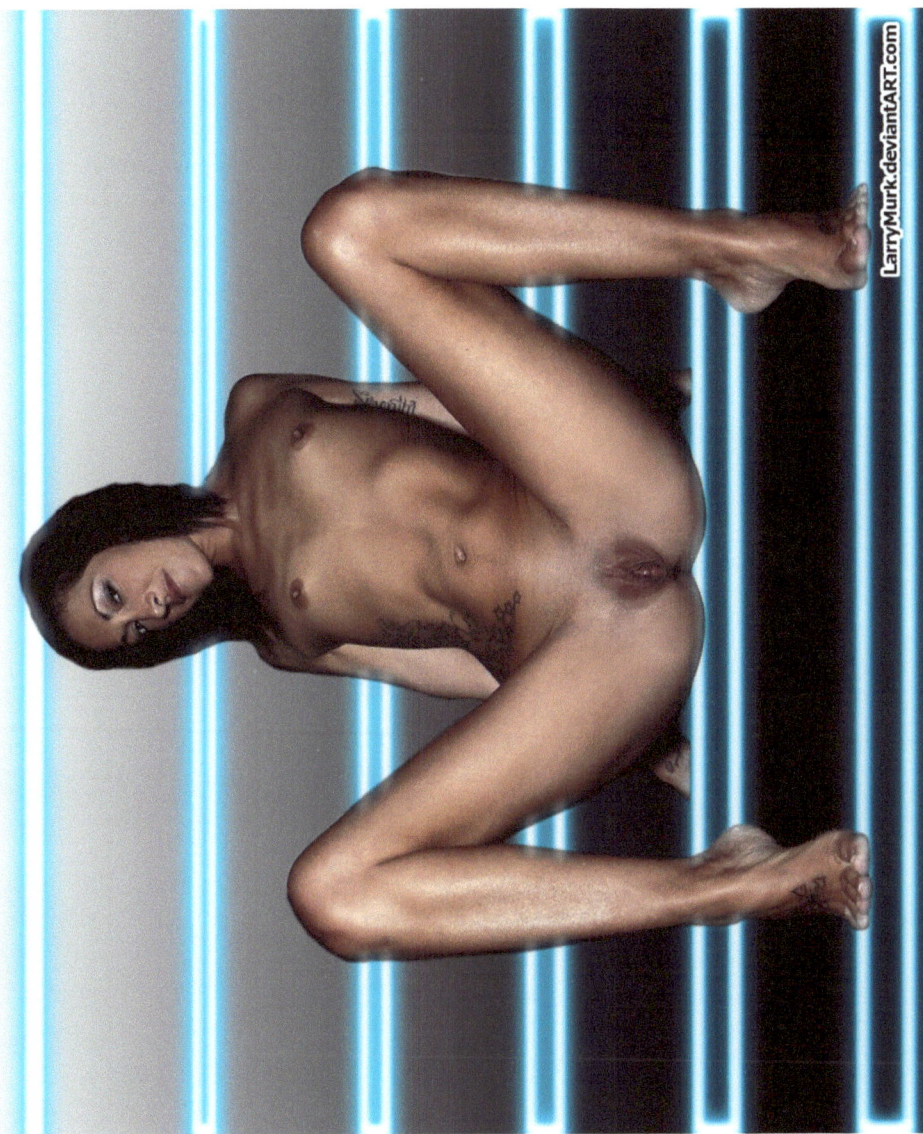

Sea Nymph

A sea nymph rests casually on the sandy ocean floor gazing across watery swirls.

Photographer: Pierre of Easy-Shutter
Model: Elana

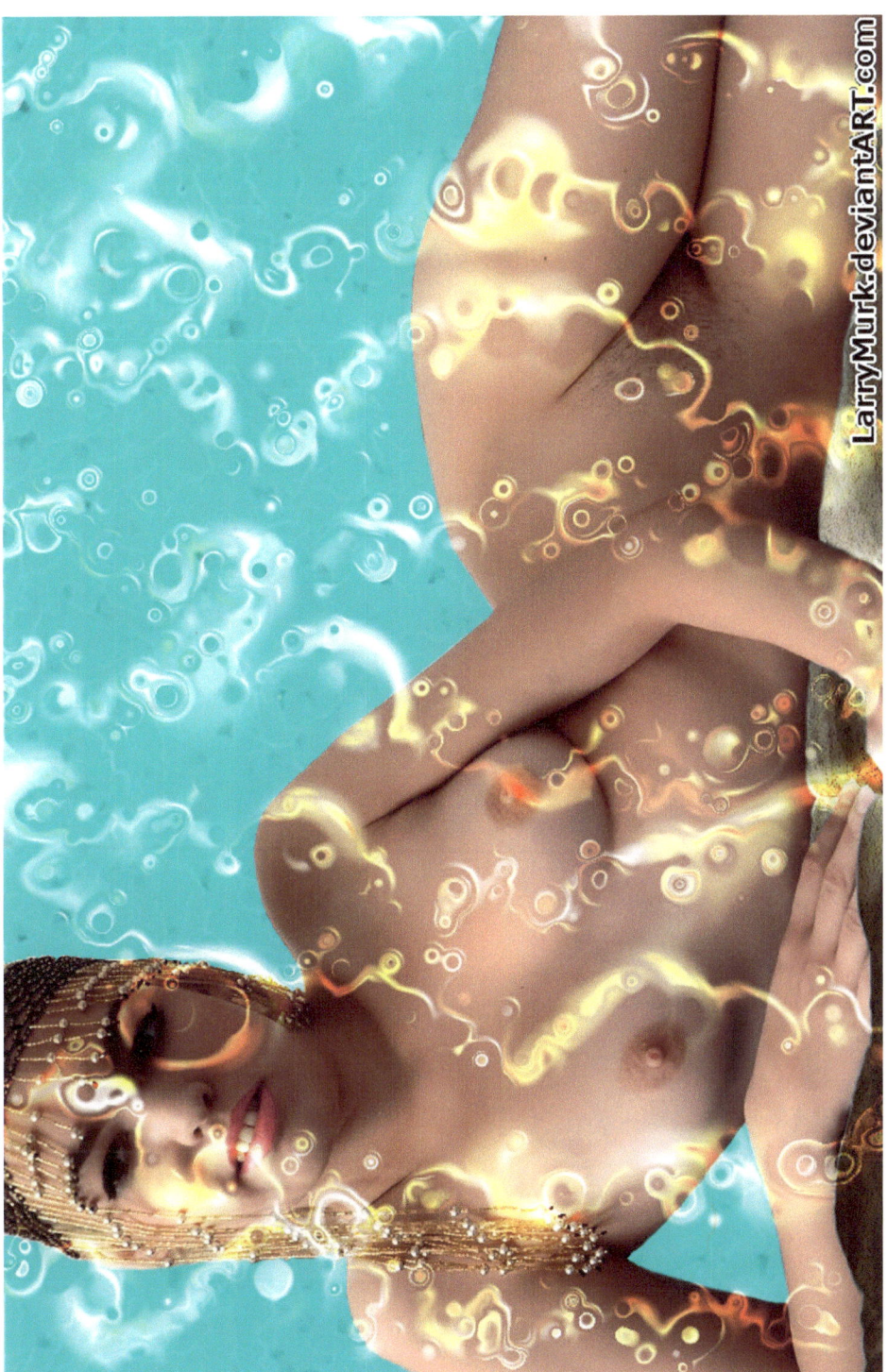

www.ingramcontent.com/pod-product-compliance
Lightning Source LLC
Chambersburg PA
CBHW040814200526
45159CB00022B/990